I Wonder Why

Records Are Broken

and Other Questions About Amazing Facts and Figures

Simon Adams

KINGFISHER

First published 2009 by Kingfisher
an imprint of Macmillan Children's Books
a division of Macmillan Publishers Ltd
The Macmillan Building, 4 Crinan Street,
London N1 9XW
Basingstoke and Oxford
Associated companies throughout the world
www.panmacmillan.com

ISBN 978-0-7534-1774-4

9 8 7 6 5 4 3 2 1
1TR/0309/SHENS/PICA/126.6MA

A CIP catalogue record for this book is available
from the British Library.

Printed in Taiwan

Illustrations by Planman Technologies (India) PVT
Ltd; cartoons by Peter Wilks.

CONTENTS

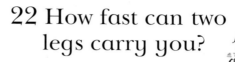

When does a record become a record?

Everything that can be measured in some way becomes a record. We can measure the length, width, height, weight, size, quantity, age, speed or volume of almost everything in the human and natural world, and keep the results as a record.

● Some records are kept for a very long time. The weather has to be recorded in the same place every day for 30 years before we know what the climate is like.

● Not every record is serious. There is a record for eating baked beans quickly!

Why do we keep track?

We all keep records. We keep a record of when the sun rises and sets every day so we know what will happen on the same day next year. We keep records so that we know what to aim for – how much higher to jump, or faster to run. And we keep records for fun!

Why are records broken?

Records are broken because people run faster and live longer, giant tortoises get older, winds blow stronger, and temperatures rise even higher and drop even lower. Each time a new extreme record is achieved, an old record is broken.

● American athlete Mildred 'Babe' Zaharias set three new world records at the high jump, javelin and hurdles in 1930–32. She also won four major golf titles and became a championship basketball player.

Which hurricane blew the hardest?

In October 2005, Hurricane Wilma blew around the Gulf of Mexico, North America, with wind speeds of up to 295km/h. It killed a total of 23 people in the Caribbean, Mexico and the USA.

● Hurricanes are named in alphabetical order, with a girl's name alternating with a boy's name.

Which records can blow you away?

Wind is a stream of air that moves from one place to another. The strength the wind blows is measured on the Beaufort scale. The scale runs from Force 0 to Force 12.

Force 2 is a light breeze.

Force 8 is a gale.

Force 12 is a hurricane.

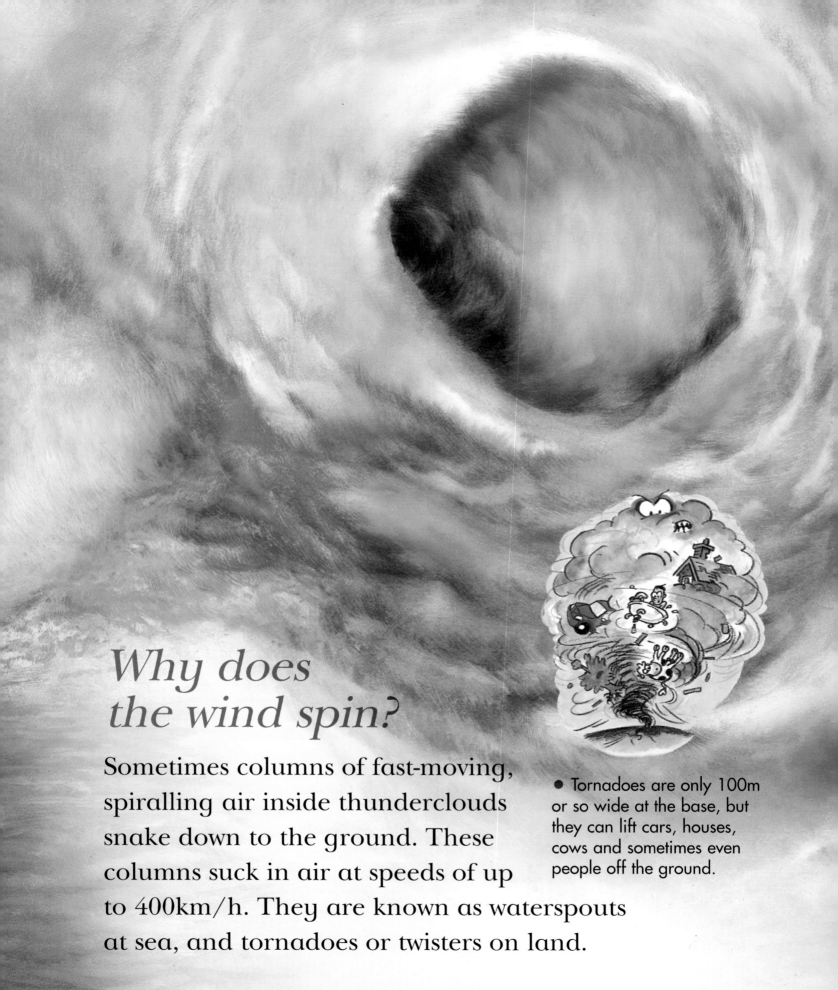

Why does the wind spin?

Sometimes columns of fast-moving, spiralling air inside thunderclouds snake down to the ground. These columns suck in air at speeds of up to 400km/h. They are known as waterspouts at sea, and tornadoes or twisters on land.

● Tornadoes are only 100m or so wide at the base, but they can lift cars, houses, cows and sometimes even people off the ground.

Where do you most need an umbrella?

The wettest place on Earth is Mawsynram in India. It rains an average of 11,870mm every year, most of it during the monsoon season. The most continuously rainy place in the world is Mount Waialeale, Hawaii, where it rains for about 350 days every year.

When do you need to wear a hard hat?

● Hail is formed when water droplets freeze to form ice. The frozen lumps then fall as hail.

A hard hat might be handy in Aurora, Nebraska, USA. The world's largest hailstone, measuring 178mm across, fell there on 22 June 2003. It is reported that hailstones killed 92 people in Bangladesh on 14 April 1986, and 25 people were killed in Henan Province, China, on 19 July 2002.

How heavily can the snow fall?

An amazing 31,102mm of snow fell on Mount Rainier in the USA, from 19 February 1971 to 18 February 1972. That is about the same height as 19 people standing on each other's heads!

● The hottest place on Earth is around lightning, when the air is briefly heated to about 30,000°C, which is five times hotter than the surface of the Sun.

Where on Earth sizzles the most?

On 13 September 1922, the temperature at Al'Aziziyah in the Libyan desert reached 57.8°C. At Dallol in Ethiopia, the temperature averaged 34.4°C for six years from 1960.

Where do angels fall?

Angel Falls, in Venezuela, South America, is the world's tallest waterfall, measuring 979m. On its way down, the wind blows much of the water into mist. About 17 million litres of water per second pours over the Boyoma Falls in Africa.

How deep is the deepest fresh water?

Lake Baikal in Russia is the deepest and biggest freshwater lake in the world. At its deepest, it reaches 1,637m below the surface. It holds more than one-fifth of the world's fresh water.

Which river is the longest?

If you were to unwind the River Nile in Africa and measure its length from its source to the sea, you would discover that it is 6,650km long. That makes it the longest river in the world, just 250km longer than the River Amazon in South America.

When was an ice cube like Jamaica?

● Only about one-tenth of an iceberg is visible above the sea's surface. The rest lurks under the water.

In 2000, iceberg B-15 broke off from the Ross Ice Shelf in Antarctica. It measured 295km long and 37km wide, making it almost the same size as the island of Jamaica in the Caribbean. It probably weighed about 3,000 million tonnes.

Which mountain towers over the world?

If you reach the top of Mount Everest, you are standing on the highest mountain in the world. Everest, in the Himalayas, Asia, is 8,850m high. Thirteen of its neighbours are also more than 8,000m high. They tower over every other mountain in the world.

● The height of Mount Everest is measured from sea level. If you measure from the seabed, the world's highest mountain is Mauna Kea in Hawaii, at 10,203m high.

Who first climbed the highest mountains?

The Italian climber Reinhold Messner was the first person to climb all 14 of the world's highest mountains above 8,000m. He climbed the first peak in 1970 and the last in 1986. In 1978, he became the first person to climb Mount Everest without bottled oxygen.

Movement of plate upwards

Mountain range

Are mountains getting bigger?

Mountains get taller. They sit on top of vast plates or slabs of rock the size of a continent. These plates float on top of the liquid insides of the Earth. Sometimes they bump into each other, making one plate rise up. This causes a mountain such as Everest to rise at about 4mm a year.

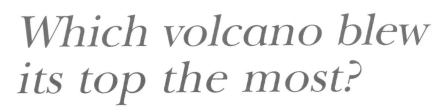

Which volcano blew its top the most?

On 27 August 1883, Krakatoa in Indonesia exploded with a bang that could be heard 4,800km from the site. It threw rocks 55km up into the sky, and dust fell as far as 5,330km away over the next 10 days. More than 36,380 people were killed.

● Earthquakes send out shock waves that travel through the ground. The wave size is measured on the Richter scale. The biggest earthquake on the scale (9) is a billion times greater than the smallest (0).

What gives the Earth the shakes?

An earthquake is a sudden movement in the Earth's surface, often caused by a fault in the crust. The worst one occurred in Shaanxi, China, on 23 January 1556. It measured 8 on the Richter scale and killed 830,000 people.

How do waves get as tall as houses?

Earthquakes, volcanic eruptions and landslides can cause huge waves to form out at sea. These tsunami can travel at speeds of up to 800km/h. The world's deadliest struck the Indian Ocean on Boxing Day 2004, killing more than 225,000 people.

● Some volcanoes erupt continuously. Kilauea in Hawaii has been active since 1983, throwing out 5 cubic metres of lava every second.

Which continent contains the most countries?

Africa contains more countries than any other continent – 53 of the world's 194 countries are found here. Many African countries are very new. In 1950, there were only 82 separate countries in the whole world.

- There are 43 landlocked countries in the world, with no direct link to the sea. Two – Liechtenstein in Europe and Uzbekistan in Asia – are double landlocked. Their peoples go through two other countries in order to reach the seaside.

Tunisia
Morocco
Western Sahara
Algeria
Mauritania
Niger
Mali
Senegal
Cameroon
Gambia
Nigeria
Guinea-Bissau
Guinea
Sierra Leone
Liberia
Ivory Coast
Ghana
Equatorial Guinea
Gabon
Congo
Angola
Namibia

- The world's population is rising at roughly 2.5 people per second, 216,000 per day, and 1,512,000 per week!

Just how crowded is planet Earth?

In 2008, the world's population was roughly 6,724,400,000 people. That is around 45 people in every square kilometre. Six out of every ten of those people live in Asia, most of them in the big cities of China, India and Japan.

Which is the most crowded country?

Monaco in southern Europe is famous for its motor racing, but it is also the most crowded country in the world. Its 32,671 people are packed into less than two square kilometres. In comparison, only 1.7 people live in each square kilometre of Mongolia.

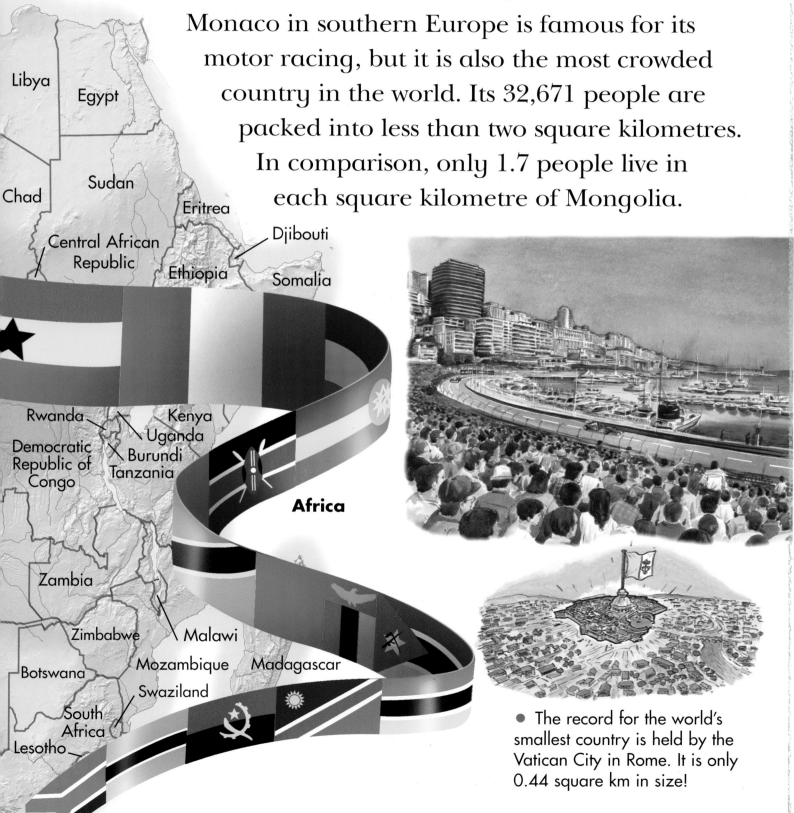

Africa

● The record for the world's smallest country is held by the Vatican City in Rome. It is only 0.44 square km in size!

How quickly can you sail round the world?

The quickest time a boat has sailed round the world without stopping is 50 days, 16 hours and 20 minutes. This record time was achieved in March 2005 by the French sailor Bruno Peyron and his crew of 13 on board the giant catamaran *Orange II*.

● The first person to sail single-handed round the world without stopping was the British sailor Robin Knox-Johnston in 1968–69. It took him 313 days.

Orange II

B-29 refuelling tanker

Refuelling hose

Lucky Lady II

Which non-stop flight set the pace?

The first plane to fly non-stop round the world was the US Air Force B-50 bomber *Lucky Lady II*. The journey, in March 1949, took 94 hours, 1 minute, and the plane refuelled four times in mid-air. *Lucky Lady II* had 13 crew on board.

● In 1960 the US Navy nuclear submarine *Triton* became the first craft to sail underwater round the world.

Who accidentally set a new record?

In 1519, Ferdinand Magellan set a new record when he sailed west from Spain across the Atlantic and Pacific oceans to the Philippines. After he died there, Sebastian de Elcano and 17 crew sailed the *Vittoria* home again, becoming the first people to sail round the world.

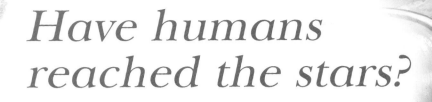

Have humans reached the stars?

Between 1969 and 1972, 12 American astronauts landed on the Moon and another 12 flew round the back of the Moon. No one has reached the stars. Unmanned spacecraft, however, have left the Solar System and flown towards the nearest stars.

● Humans can only survive underwater without breathing for about nine minutes and can descend to about 200m. Emperor penguins can reach a depth of 265m, while sperm whales frequently dive to 1,200m.

How deep have humans sunk?

The deepest place on Earth is the Challenger Deep at the bottom of the Mariana Trench in the Pacific Ocean. On 23 January 1960, the bathyscaphe *Trieste* descended 10,911m to the trench floor.

It is not just humans that have flown in space. Cats, dogs, monkeys, frogs, spiders, worms, snails, fish, rats, mice and other creatures have all made the journey.

How fast can you cross a desert?

Someone has gone at an incredible 1,228km/h, which is faster than the speed of sound! This record was set in the Black Rock Desert in Nevada, USA, by Andy Green on 15 October 1997. His jet-propelled car *Thrust SSC* flew along at 20.5km a minute.

The fastest a person has ever cycled over 200m is 9.772 seconds, which is about 20.5m per second.

Can you jump like a flea?

A flea can jump 130 times its own height, but the record for an adult male human is only 2.45m and an adult woman 2.09m – both less than twice the average human height. Even using a pole, an adult man can only vault 6.14m, or three times a man's average height.

● People can jump four to five times their own length. The current world record for the long jump is 8.95m.

How fast can two legs carry you?

The fastest man on two legs over 100m is Usain Bolt, a Jamaican athlete. At the Beijing Olympic Games in 2008, he ran the course in 9.69 seconds, a new world record. The record for women, 10.49 seconds, was set by an American sprinter called Florence Griffith-Joyner in 1988.

One sport not included in the decathlon is mobile phone throwing. A world championship has been held in Finland every year since 2000.

Women compete in the eight events of the heptathlon. It is like the decathlon, only with one less track race and no discus-throwing event.

Which is the sportiest sport?

In the decathlon, athletes compete in 10 different sports over two days. On day one they complete the 100m sprint, the long jump, shot put, high jump and 400m. On day two they complete the 110m hurdles, the discus, pole vault and javelin before finishing with a 1,500m race.

Which is the world's biggest city?

Tokyo, Japan, is the biggest city in the world. About 32,450,000 people live there. Seoul in South Korea and Mexico City are the next two biggest cities, with around 20,500,000 people each.

● Some suspension bridges are so long that their two towers point slightly away from each other. This is because the surface of the Earth is curved.

Who are the greatest tunnellers?

At the moment, the greatest tunnel builders are the Japanese. Their 53.8km-long Seikhan railway tunnel links Honshu and Hokkaido islands. In 2017, the Swiss Gotthard Base Tunnel under the Alps will be open. That will be an amazing 57.1km long.

How high do we build?

The tallest inhabited building in the world is the Taipei 101 Tower in Taiwan, with its 101 floors. When the Burj Dubai ('Dubai Tower'), in the United Arab Emirates, opens in 2009, it will dwarf every other structure in the world at 818m.

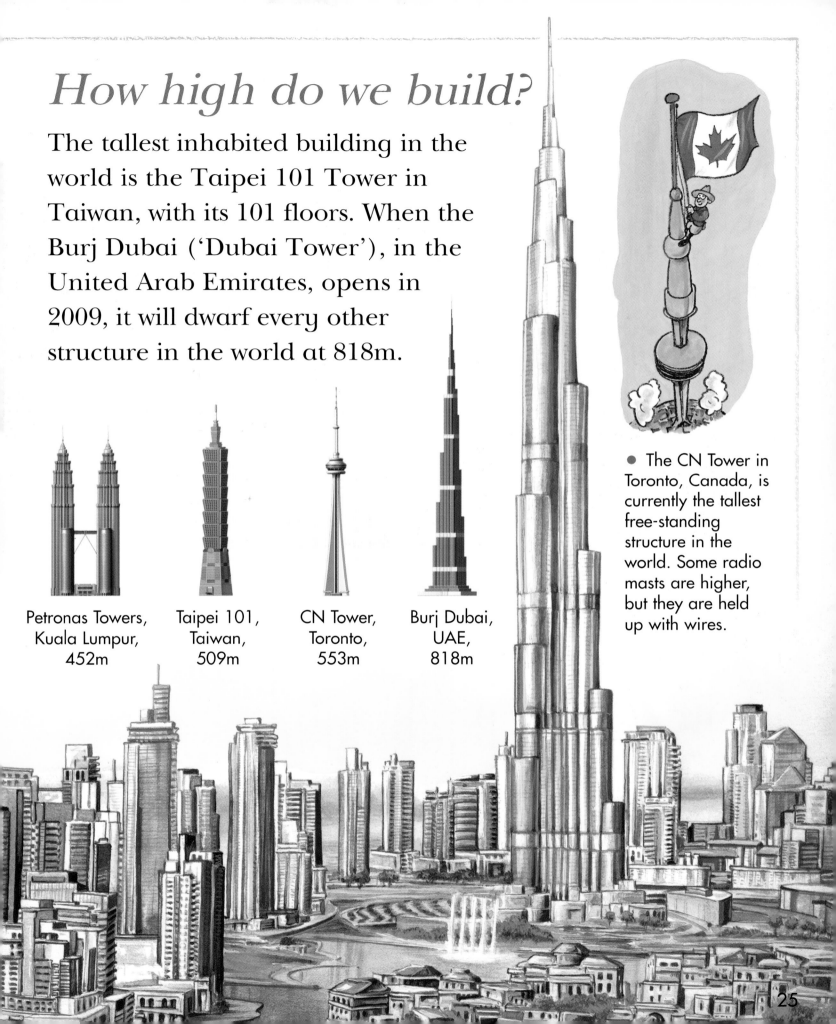

Petronas Towers, Kuala Lumpur, 452m

Taipei 101, Taiwan, 509m

CN Tower, Toronto, 553m

Burj Dubai, UAE, 818m

● The CN Tower in Toronto, Canada, is currently the tallest free-standing structure in the world. Some radio masts are higher, but they are held up with wires.

25

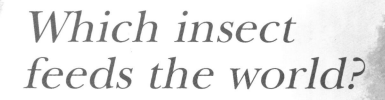

Which insect feeds the world?

Honeybees are the only insects that provide food which humans can eat. They make honey to feed themselves in winter. Any leftovers are harvested by beekeepers. The bees visit up to five million flowers to make 1kg of honey.

● Baby blue whales grow at an amazing 90kg a day. They grow into the world's biggest creatures, weighing in at around 130 tonnes.

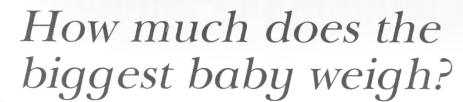

How much does the biggest baby weigh?

The blue whale gives birth to a 2,000kg whopper that is already 7m long. A human baby only weighs about 3.2kg at birth and is around 36cm long.

Where do big birds fly?

The biggest flying bird is the albatross. It lives in the Southern Ocean and the northern Pacific Ocean, and has a wingspan of 3.7m. The largest flightless bird is the 2.74m-tall ostrich, which lives in Africa.

● The tiny bee hummingbird is 5.7cm long and weighs just 1.6g, half the weight of a UK 1p coin.

Which animals are the speediest?

The fastest creature in the world is the peregrine falcon, which dives at speeds of up to 298km/h. On land, the cheetah is quickest, racing along at 105km/h. Some humans can manage 37km/h over 100m.

● The Arctic tern flies from the Arctic to the Antarctic and back again every year, a round trip of 40,000km.

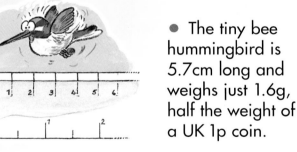

Which shark is a gentle giant?

The whale shark is the biggest fish in the world. It grows up to 12m long and can weigh 21 tonnes. Yet this vast beast is harmless to humans and other fish. It eats only plankton, the tiny plants, animals and bacteria that drift around in the sea.

How big do snakes' appetites get?

An African rock python will easily swallow a 59kg antelope. Reticulated pythons eat pigs weighing 60kg and more. And one 5.17m-long python once ate a 14 year-old Malay boy.

● The coastal taipan snake of Australia is so deadly that its venom could kill 120 people.

Which hairy spider is a goliath?

The goliath bird-eating spider lives in the South American rainforest. It is as big as a dinner plate, with legs up to 25cm long. It eats birds and other small creatures, and is harmless to humans, although it can sting.

● The banana spider of Central and South America lives hidden in bunches of bananas. It produces enough venom to kill six adults.

Giant storm known as
the Great Red Spot

● Light travels at an amazing
300,000km per second. Even
at that speed, sunshine is
8 minutes, 17 seconds old
when we see it. Light from
our nearest star takes
4.22 years to reach us.

Planets
only

● There used to be nine
planets in our Solar System,
but in 2006 Pluto was
downgraded to become
a 'dwarf planet'.

Which planet is king?

Jupiter is the biggest planet in our
Solar System. The planet is 142,984km
wide. It is so big that it is 2.5 times the
size of all the other seven planets in
the Solar System added together.
The planet is named after Jupiter,
Roman king of the gods.

How brightly can a star shine?

The brightest star we can see is our Sun, because it is the closest one to us. But the brightest star we can see from Earth in the night sky is Sirius, which is also called the Dog Star. It is more than 20 times brighter than our Sun.

Can we measure a galaxy?

A galaxy is a large group of stars held together by gravity. We measure the size of a galaxy by how long light takes to travel from one side to the other. The Abell 2029 galaxy is 5.6 million light years wide, 56 times wider than our Milky Way galaxy (above).

Index

KEY TO MEASUREMENTS	
°C	degrees centigrade
cm	centimetre
km	kilometre
km/h	kilometres per hour
kg	kilogram
m	metre
mm	millimetre